W9-AOW-179

The Sayings of Evelyn Waugh

The Sayings of

EVELYN
WAUGH

edited by
Donat Gallagher

DUCKWORTH

First published in 1996 by
Gerald Duckworth & Co. Ltd.
The Old Piano Factory
48 Hoxton Square, London N1 6PB
Tel: 0171 729 5986
Fax: 0171 729 0015

A catalogue record for this book is available
from the British Library

ISBN 0 7156 2742 2

Typeset by Ray Davies
Printed in Great Britain by
Redwood Books Ltd, Trowbridge

Contents

Sources

Rossetti: His Life and Works, 1928
Decline and Fall: An Illustrated Novelette, 1928
Vile Bodies, 1930; Penguin 1961
Labels: A Mediterranean Journal, 1930
Remote People, 1931
Black Mischief, 1932
Ninety-Two Days, 1934
A Handful of Dust, 1934
Edmund Campion, 1935; 2nd ed. 1947
Waugh in Abyssinia, 1936
Scoop, 1938; Little Brown 1977
Robbery Under Law: The Mexican Object Lesson, 1939
Put Out More Flags, 1942
Brideshead Revisited, 1945 and Penguin 1960
When the Going Was Good, 1946
Wine in Peace and War, n.d.
Scott-King's Modern Europe, 1947
The Loved One: An Anglo-American Tragedy, 1948
Helena, 1950
Love Among the Ruins, 1953
The Ordeal of Gilbert Pinfold: A Conversation Piece, 1957; 1977
    [abbreviated here as *Pinfold*]
The Life of the Right Reverend Ronald Knox, 1959 [abbreviated
    here as *Knox*]
A Little Learning, 1964
Sword of Honour, 1965

The Diaries of Evelyn Waugh, ed. Michael Davie, 1976
The Letters of Evelyn Waugh, ed. Mark Amory, 1980
The Essays, Articles and Reviews of Evelyn Waugh, ed. Donat
    Gallagher, 1983
*Mr Wu and Mrs Stitch: The Letters of Evelyn Waugh and Diana
    Cooper*, ed. Artemis Cooper, 1991 [abbreviated here as *Stitch*]
Daphne Fielding, *The Nearest Way Home*, 1970

In the quotations that follow first British or Uniform editions
are cited except where indicated. Uncollected pieces are
referenced in the text.

Introduction

In an early article Evelyn Waugh identified this century's most Deadly Sin as 'too much tolerance' and noted, ominously, that there were 'still things worth fighting *against*'. The intolerable things were not only philistines, prudes and censors but, more significantly, anything that became very fashionable. Thus at the height of their popularity among the intellectuals and the smart set, Waugh satirized Modern Art, 'talking pictures', cocktails, the cult of Youth, socialism, functional architecture, the motor car, air travel, Marxist literary theory, Winston Churchill, the Russian alliance, classlessness, D.H. Lawrence, 'Change' in the Roman Catholic Church .... The conservative philosophy implicit in the attacks was overlaid early in life by avant-garde style, later by the vivid Pinfold *persona*; always by Waugh's irrepressible tendency to be funny, elegant and shocking.

Waugh's sixteen novels made a significant contribution to the art of English fiction. Between novels he usually published a travel book or a biography and a moderate amount of journalism, much of which has been collected. He was also a candid diarist, a prolific letter writer and an inspired talker; most of the diaries and several selections of letters have been printed, and his sayings are often quoted.

Waugh was keenly interested in the contemporary world: major events such as the Italo-Abyssinian conflict and the Second World War appear in the fiction and non-fiction, as do topical issues such as the marriage laws, education, class, Hollywood, the systematic corruption of public opinion by the Press, and the decline of beauty and amenity in the 'Modern World'. But his abiding loves were literature and finely produced books; art and architecture (in particular English narrative painting and domestic building); Roman Catholicism; travel; the structures and conventions of England's traditional life; and food and wine.

Well read, formidably intelligent and determined 'to think from first principles', Waugh had a sound understanding of the bases of his art and the functioning of society; although the principles are rarely discussed in an article but tend to emerge incidentally in a biography, travel book or review.

One of the finest and most versatile stylists of the century, Waugh could write 'Beachcomber' whimsy, formal rhetoric, popular invective, lively narrative and lush ornament. His exposition of the complexities involved in the Italo-Abyssinian war has justly been called a 'masterpiece of lucid compression'. But the distinctive style is elegant and pointed, subversive in intent while dead-pan in manner: ' "This is my daughter," said Dr Fagan with some disgust.' The one constant is that Waugh drew on a wide vocabulary, using each word in its precise meaning and nuance, consciously intending to give pleasure.

Underlying the turbulence of Waugh's career, and intimately related to it, runs a steady thread of artistic and philosophic development at which a summary can only hint.

Born in 1903 into a literary family, Waugh was a clever schoolboy with a talent for writing and drawing, alternately attracted to the 'forceful and flamboyant' and the contemplative and aesthetic. At Oxford, although he could have made a scholar, he joined an anarchic, mainly upper-class set and went down with a Third; but also with experience essential to his development and with friends in the social world which the novels exploit.

Several aimless years followed, punctuated by courses in art and carpentry and teaching jobs of ever-declining prestige. At his lowest point, Waugh wrote a monograph on the Pre-Raphaelite Brotherhood – he was related to Holman Hunt – for a friend's private press; Duckworth then commissioned a life of Dante Gabriel Rossetti. *Rossetti: His Life and Works* (1928) is an amusingly Stracheyan, but solid, study that quietly subverts Modernist aesthetics. In the same year Waugh married, and *Decline and Fall* burst upon the literary scene. A work of comic genius, it is also profoundly critical of the early twentieth century's art, architecture, tainted wealth and lack of belief; it signals that the author, having seen and suffered the unreason of the 'waste land', is about to set his own life in order.

Waugh now embarked on professional advancement, cultivating the smart set and writing anything – mainly about social amusements and Youth – that any high-paying editor would buy. *Labels*, a travel book containing his pioneering essay on Gaudi, appeared in 1930. But the climax to the period was *Vile Bodies* (1930), which popularized the argot of the Bright Young People and became a commercial and fashionable success.

Fortune, however, decrees that 'no one will be be very happy for very long'. Shortly before the triumph of *Vile Bodies*, Waugh's marriage broke up; shortly afterwards he joined the Roman Catholic Church. These momentous events turned him away from facile Mayfair fiction to a decade of travel and politics, and novels growing steadily more adventurous in style and profound in theme.

In 1930 Waugh capably reported the coronation of Haile

Selassie, the modernizing emperor of Ethiopia. Out of this experience came *Remote People* and a serio-comic novel, *Black Mischief*, which dramatizes the disasters inseparable from restless innovation. A grim journey through the hinterland of British Guiana in 1933 gave rise to *Ninety-Two Days* and *A Handful of Dust*, another gruesome fantasy with a profoundly conservative theme: the inability of unexamined humanism to sustain civilized life.

Religious conviction now began to deepen. Waugh wrote an admiring biography of Edmund Campion (1935), clearly identifying himself with the martyr's claim that the Christian faith is absolutely satisfactory to the mind and completely compelling to anyone who will give it 'indifferent and quiet audience'.

Also in 1935 Waugh covered the Italo-Abyssinian war for the *Daily Mail*, devoting much of his effort 'to contradicting the lies the journalists tell'. The manipulation of journalists and the conventions of reporting are analysed in *Waugh in Abyssinia* and joyfully satirized in *Scoop*.

Politically, Waugh became 'pro-Italian' to the extent that he regarded the opposition to Italy's intervention in Abyssinia as factitious, and as inevitably catastrophic for the Abyssinians. Similarly, he was 'pro-Franco' in the sense that he opposed the Republican cause. But the main battlefield of the Political Decade was literary: Waugh's hostility to Marxist theory was absolute, his reviewing relatively open: Auden and Spender were ridiculed, Isherwood and Marshal praised.

The Second World War reshaped Waugh's career. On the one hand, while a serving soldier, he published two profitable novels, *Put Out More Flags* and *Brideshead Revisited*, which brought him quite new financial and artistic independence. On the other hand the postwar settlement, which subjugated large Roman Catholic populations to Stalinist regimes aiming at their extinction, was deeply disturbing to Waugh, who had first-hand experience of the process in Jugoslavia. Like many of his co-religionists, he discovered a new loyalty and fervour at this time, and his writings became more consistently polemical and theological.

Despite its splendours, the world evoked in *Brideshead Revisited* is doomed; only faith survives. *Helena* (1950), written in defiance of contemporary taste, asserts the vital importance to Christianity of its basis in history, and finds life's meaning in the answer each individual makes to the 'call' to render some unique service. *Sword of Honour*, a trilogy of novels about the Second World War, is the culmination of Waugh's achievement. His creed has matured into a philosophy of life, tending now to compassion and resignation. While his country blunders into dishonour, Guy Crouchback is healed by carrying out acts of mercy which he, and only he, can perform.

The most popular work of the post-war period was a novel in the old black comic mode, *The Loved One* (1948), which uses an exposé of American burial customs to explore the weaknesses of American civilization.

The essays of the postwar years tend to combine religious subjects with travel, as in 'The American Epoch in the Catholic Church', 'The Defence of the Holy Places' or 'Half in Love with Easeful Death'. Others were about co-religionists such as Graham Greene and J.F. Powers. During the 1950s Waugh also became a belligerent champion of Roman Catholic causes.

Postwar egalitarianism dismayed Waugh because he held the unseasonable view that all successful societies had been blessed by a system of classes. *Scott-King's Modern Europe* (1947), set in Franco's Spain, mocks the 'modern two-class State of officials and proletariat'. *Love among the Ruins* (1953) is a bitter dystopia about England under Welfare. Reaction to this novel was extreme and provoked Waugh to new levels of offence. His public *persona* swelled: to many he was a snobbish ogre, to others a champion of England's traditional life; in either case the natural choice of an editor in search of a Tory provocateur who, whether loved or loathed, was irresistibly readable. *The Ordeal of Gilbert Pinfold* records a period of madness in Waugh's life and frankly analyses the public *persona*.

In 1958 Waugh published an outstanding biography of Mgr Ronald Knox, emphasising his distinction as a scholar and stylist. This was part of a campaign to have theological writing recognized as mainstream literature. The biography also reveals something of Waugh's dislike of ecclesiastical authorities, which was consistent with the mild anticlericalism and liberalism of 'The American Epoch in the Catholic Church' (1949). Nevertheless, at the time of the Vatican Council, when liberalism seemed to threaten fundamental doctrine, Waugh embarked on the most vehement and sustained campaign of his career, an attack on 'Change' in the Roman Catholic Church.

Evelyn Waugh has given more delight through brilliant comic invention and dazzling style than any other serious novelist of the century, while his courage and prescience earn increasing respect. He refused 'to go flopping along' with fashion, and since his death opinion has been steadily catching him up.

On Himself

Save for a few uncertain flashes my mind is dark in the years of illiteracy; or rather, save for a few pale shadows it is an even glow of pure happiness.

Little Learning, 28

Now, that summer term with Sebastian, it seemed as though I was being given a brief spell of happy childhood, and though its toys were silk shirts and liqueurs and cigars and its naughtiness high in the catalogue of grave sins, there was something of nursery freshness about us that fell little short of the joy of innocence.

Brideshead, 41

I had warned my father that my *viva* might mean a second. It meant a third, and I was overcome with regret, not, I am ashamed to say, for the giddy nights, but for the sober ones. I had not done much work, but I had done some. Had I known I was only to get a third I would not have wasted my time.

Sunday Dispatch, 10 July 1938

My next plan was to be a carpenter, and for a winter I went regularly to classes in a government polytechnic. Those were delightful days, under the tuition of a brilliant but speechless little cabinet-maker who could explain nothing and demonstrate everything. To see him cutting concealed dovetails gave me a thrill which, I suppose, others get from seeing their favourite batsman at the wicket or bull fighter in the ring.

Essays, 191

There are only two sorts of job always open under the English social system – domestic service and education. However abominable one's record, though one may be fresh from prison or the lunatic asylum, one can always look after the silver or teach the young. I had not the right presence for a footman, so I chose the latter.

Ibid.

Dickens held it against his parents that they tried to force him into a blacking factory instead of letting him write. The last firm at which I solicited a job was engaged in the manufacture of blacking. I pleaded. If I wasn't employed I should be driven to Literature. But the Manager was relentless. It was no use my thinking of blacking. I must write a book.

Ibid., 191-2

I did not know it was possible to be so miserable and live.
(Written after the break-up of his first marriage.) *Letters*, 39

On firm intellectual conviction but with little emotion I was admitted into the Roman Catholic Church .... I look back aghast at the presumption with which I thought myself suitable for reception and with wonder at the trust of the priest who saw the possibility of growth in such a dry soul.

Essays, 368

I did not really know where I was going, so, when anyone asked me I said to Russia. Thus my trip started, like an autobiography, upon a rather nicely qualified basis of falsehood and self-glorification.

Labels, 9

I envy among my friends this one's adaptability to diverse company, this one's cosmopolitan experience, this one's impenetrable armour against sentimentality and humbug, this one's freedom from conventional prejudices, and realise that, whatever happens to me and however I deplore it, I shall never in fact become a 'hardboiled man of the world'; that I shall always be ill at ease with nine out of every ten people I meet; that I shall always find something startling and rather abhorrent in the things most other people think worth doing, and something puzzling in their standards of importance; that I shall probably be increasingly vulnerable to the inevitable minor disasters and injustices of life.

Remote People, 110-11

I can't advise you [to marry me] because I think it would be beastly for you, but think how nice it would be for me. I am restless & moody & misanthropic & lazy and have no money except what I earn and if I got ill you would starve. In fact it's a lousy proposition.

(To Laura, his second wife.) *Letters*, 104

My 39th birthday. A good year. I have begotten a fine daughter, published a successful book, drunk 300 bottles of red wine and smoked 300 or more Havana cigars. I have got back to soldiering among friends. I get steadily worse as a soldier with the passage of time, but more patient and humble – as far as soldiering is concerned. I have about 900 pounds in hand and no grave debts except to the Government; health excellent except when impaired by wine; a wife I love, agreeable work in surroundings of great beauty. Well that is as much as one can hope for. *Diaries*, 530

I went to General Thomas's headquarters for a week's trial – today returned unaccepted. This is a great relief. The primary lack of sympathy seemed to come from my being slightly drunk in the mess on the first evening. I told him I could not change the habits of a lifetime for a whim of his.
Ibid., 559

Mr Pinfold was neither a scholar nor a regular soldier; the part for which he cast himself was a combination of eccentric don and testy colonel and he acted it strenuously, before his children at Lychpole and his cronies in London, until it came to dominate his whole outward personality. When he ceased to be alone, when he swung into his club or stumped up the nursery stairs, he left half of himself behind, and the other half swelled to fill its place. He offered the world a front of pomposity mitigated by indiscretion, that was as hard, bright, and antiquated as a cuirass. *Pinfold*, 15

My chief sorrow at the moment is that, as all epigrams get attributed to Ronnie Knox, all rudeness gets attributed to me. Beasts come to me and say: 'I heard something so amusing you said the other day' and then recount an act of hideous boorishness without the shadow of reality.
Stitch, 150

I'm still a pure aesthete! But in middle life one doesn't have to dress up in special clothes to enjoy architecture, you know.
BBC, 20 July 1960

The tiny kindling of charity which came to Mr Pinfold through his religion sufficed only to temper his disgust and change it to boredom. *Pinfold*, 14

'Damn. Damn. Damn. Why does everyone except me find it so easy to be nice.' *Ibid.*, 31

I have no bloody recreations. I do not hunt. I do not fish. I do not kill animals.

Sunday Telegraph 1964

The only reason a writer lives in a large quiet country house is that he wants – quiet. This is no country gentleman's house. It is not full of servants, it is full of children and grandchildren.

Ibid.

INTERVIEWER: What do you feel is your worst fault?
WAUGH: Irritability … with absolutely everything. Inanimate objects and people, animals, anything.

BBC, 20 July 1960

Education

The splendid thing about Education is that everyone wants it and, like influenza, you can give it away without losing any of it yourself.   *Essays*, 10

Unsystematic discipline varying with the mood of the household makes a far better training for life than the wisest code of rules. It is very bewildering for the old-fashioned child, brought up to a system of rigid justice and reasoned recompense, to find himself plunged into a world where things are less logically operated. The modern mother will see just as much of her children as she finds amusing and they will thus learn the excellent principle that they must make themselves agreeable if they want attention.

Evening Standard, 8 April 1929

Boys between the ages of thirteen and eighteen are completely odious creatures, destructive of peace and property, uncouth, self-assertive, and generally unsuited to civilized company. Accordingly parents have to find a race of men so desperate and mercenary that they will devote their lives to keeping them away from home during the greater part of this period.

Daily Mail, 30 August 1930

'I expect you'll be becoming a schoolmaster, sir. That's what most of the gentlemen does, sir, that gets sent down for indecent behaviour.'

Decline and Fall, 19

The private schools of England are to the educated classes what the Union Workhouses are to the very poor. Relief is granted to all who come but it is provided in as unpalatable a form as possible.   *Essays*, 51

'I have been in the scholastic profession long enough to know that nobody enters it unless he has some very good reason which he is anxious to conceal.'

Decline and Fall, 26

'We schoolmasters must temper discretion with deceit.'

Ibid., 33

'This looks like being the first end of term I've seen for two years,' Grimes said dreamily. 'Funny thing, I can always get on all right for about six weeks, and then I land in the soup. I don't believe I was ever meant by Nature to be a schoolmaster. Temperament,' said Grimes, with a far away look in his eyes – 'that's been my trouble, temperament and sex.'

Ibid., 37

'Meanwhile you will write an essay on "self-indulgence". There will be a prize of half a crown for the longest essay, irrespective of any possible merit.'

Ibid., 49

The more influential and intelligent young schoolmasters came [back from the Great War] with their own faith sadly shaken in those very standards they had fought to preserve. They returned with a jolly tolerance of everything that seemed 'modern'. Every effort was made to encourage the children at the public schools to 'think for themselves'. When they should have been whipped and taught Greek paradigms, they were set arguing about birth control and nationalization. Their crude little opinions were treated with respect. It is hardly surprising that they were Bolshevik at 18 and bored at 20.

Essays, 61

To know and love one other human being is the root of all wisdom.

Brideshead, 41

All the wickedness of that time was like the spirit they mix with the pure grape of the Douro, heady stuff full of dark ingredients; it at once enriched and retarded the whole process of adolescence as the spirit checks the fermentation of the wine.

Ibid.

Do Oxford and Cambridge maintain a tradition of genuine culture? To judge by the blank faces and blanker conversation in a London ballroom one would suspect that they did not. To judge by the decoration of my tutor's rooms, one would say with certainty that they did not. Oxford is not up to date in the latest theories of aesthetics and psychology from Berlin and Paris. As far as direct monetary rewards are considered, our parents would have done far better to have packed us off to Monte Carlo to try our luck at the tables.

Essays, 83

Those who choose or are obliged to begin regular, remunerative responsible work at the moment they leave school, particularly if they have a had a fairly carefully tended adolescence, often show signs of arrested development. It is just because Oxford keeps them back from their careers that it is of most value.   *Ibid.*, 84

Oxford – submerged now and obliterated, irrecoverable as Lyonness, so quickly have the waters come flooding in – Oxford, in those days, was still a city of aquatint. In her spacious and quiet streets men walked and spoke as they had done in Newman's day; her autumnal mists, her grey springtime, and the rare glory of her summer days – such as that day – when the chestnut was in flower and the bells rang out high and clear over her gables and cupolas, exhaled the soft vapours of a thousand years of learning. It was this cloistral hush which gave our laughter its resonance, and carried it still, joyously, over the intervening clamour.   *Brideshead*, 20

We have lost sight of the simple fact that there are as many different kinds of education as there are human activities. A sailor, a priest, a groom, or an ambassador is an educated man in so far as he has mastered his own art. A cabinet maker who really knows his trade, can handle his tools with the precision of a surgeon, can pick his timber with the eye of a connoisseur and can impart his skill in the workshop, is a supremely well educated man even if he cannot read and write.
                                            Sunday Dispatch, 10 June 1938

The sense of period is a product of the English public school and University education; it is, in fact, almost its only product which cannot be acquired far better and far more cheaply elsewhere …. I am inclined to think that it is practically valueless. It consists of a vague knowledge of History, Literature, and Art, an amateurish interest in architecture and costume, of social, religious and political institutions, of drama, of the biographies of the chief characters of each century, and of a few memorable anecdotes and jokes, scraps of diaries and correspondence and family history. All these snacks and titbits of scholarship become fused together into a more or less homogeneous and consistent whole, so that the cultured Englishman has a sense of the past, in a continuous series of clear and pretty *tableaux vivants*.   *Labels*, 40

Anyone who has been to an English public school will always feel comparatively at home in prison.   *Decline and Fall*, 221

Literary Life

Of all the Arts the one most to be recommended to the young beginner is literature. Painting is messy; music is noisy; and the applied arts and crafts all require a certain amount of skill. But writing is clean, quiet, and can be done anywhere at any time by anyone.   *Essays*, 48

I know what you [Henry Yorke] mean about purple patches. My new book [*Vile Bodies*] is black with them – but then I live by my pen as they say and you don't.

Letters, 37

The average sophisticated novelist sits down to earn his fifteen, twenty or twenty-five guineas from the penny daily in a mood of apology. He hopes that his friends will not see the article, and he puts in several sly allusions to make clear to any who do that his tongue is in his cheek. He tries to secure the rewards of popular acclamation while remaining aloof from popular sympathy. Lawrence plunged into the work of 'feature' journalism with all the gusto of a prophet.

Essays, 71

For prestige it would be good to make A Handful of Dust long but one has to think about the book and not the reviewers. What I have done is excellent. I don't think it could be better. Very gruesome. Rather like Webster in modern idiom ...

Stitch, 43

I am going to give up the snobbish attempt I have made for some years to be low-brow and [resolve] to be just as fastidious as my nature allows, to read books again as I used before my 1928 debacle. Then to be sober often ...

Ibid., 57

Certain trades and classes seek personal publicity; not so respectable writers, for their entire vocation is one of self-expression and it seems obvious to them that if they cannot make themselves understood in years of laborious writing, they will not succeed in a few minutes of conversation. So when we see interviewers advancing, we fly.

Essays, 371

A writer must face the choice of becoming an artist or a prophet. He can shut himself up at his desk and selfishly seek pleasure in perfecting his own skill or he can pace about, dictating dooms and exhortations on the topics of the day. The recluse at the desk has a chance of giving abiding pleasure to other; the publicist has none at all.

Ibid., 481

All the penalties of eminence which real writers shirk Mr Spender pays with enthusiasm and they may very well be grateful to him. In middle age he forms a valuable dummy who draws off the bores while they get on with their work.

Ibid., 395

Humility is not a virtue propitious to the artist. It is often pride, emulation, avarice, malice – all odious qualities – which drive a man to complete, elaborate, refine, destroy, renew, his work until he has made something that gratifies his pride and envy and greed. And in doing so he enriches the world more than the generous and good, though he may lose his own soul in the process. That is the paradox of artistic achievement.

Ibid., 560

The contemporary English literary world may be conveniently divided into those who can write but cannot think, those who can think but cannot write, and those who can neither think nor write but employ themselves at international congresses lecturing on the predicament of the writer in modern society.

Ibid., 600

'Creative' is an invidious term often used at the expense of the critic. A better word, except that it would always involve explanation, would be 'architectural'. I believe that what makes a writer, as distinct from a clever and cultured man who can write, is an added energy and breadth of vision which enables him to conceive and complete a structure.

Ibid., 238

Literature & Film

Literature is the right use of language irrespective of the subject or reason of the utterance. A political speech may be, and sometimes is, literature; a sonnet to the moon may be, and often is, trash.

Essays, 478

Properly understood style is not a seductive decoration added to a functional structure; it is of the essence of a work of art.

Ibid.

Firbank is the first quite modern writer to solve for himself the aesthetic problem of representation in fiction …. Other solutions are offered for the problem, but in them the author has been forced into a subjective attitude to his material; Firbank remained objective and emphasized the fact which his contemporaries were neglecting that the novel should be directed for entertainment. This is the debt which the present generation owes to him.

Ibid., 59

Technically, *Living* is without exception the most interesting book I have read …. The effects which Mr [Henry] Green wishes to make and the information he wishes to give are so accurately and subtly conceived that it becomes necessary to take language one step further than its grammatical limits allow.

Ibid., 81-2

A danger in novel-writing is to make one's immediate effect and then discard the means employed. Modern novelists taught by Mr James Joyce are at last realizing the importance of re-echoing and remodifying the same themes.

Ibid., 82

There is a lurking puritanism at Cambridge (England) and in many parts of the New World, which is ever ready to condemn pleasure even in its purest form.

Ibid., 478

James Joyce was a writer possessed by style. His later work lost almost all faculty of communication, so intimate, allusive and idiosyncratic did it become, so obsessed by euphony and nuance. But because he was obscure and can only be read with intense intellectual effort – and therefore without easy pleasure – he is admitted into the academic canon.

Ibid.

The necessary elements of style are lucidity, elegance, individuality; these three qualities combine to form a preservative which ensures the nearest approximation to permanence in the fugitive world of letters.

Ibid.

Lucidity does not imply universal intelligibility. Henry James is the most lucid of writers, but not the simplest .... The test of lucidity is whether the statement can be read as meaning anything other than what it intends.

Ibid.

Lactantius delighted in writing, in the joinery and embellishment of his sentences, in the consciousness of high rare virtue when every word had been used in its purest and most precise sense, in the kitten games of syntax and rhetoric. Words could do anything except generate their own meanings.

Helena, 120

I regard writing not as an investigation of character, but as an exercise in the use of language, and with this I am obsessed. I have no technical psychological interest. It is drama, speech and events that interest me.

Paris Review, no. 8, 1963

One reads Somerset Maugham with a feeling of increasing respect for the mastery of his trade. One has the same delight as in watching a first-class cabinet maker cutting dovetails; in the days of bakelite that is a rare and bewitching experience. He is, I believe, the only living studio-master under whom one can study with profit. He has no marked idiosyncrasies which threaten the pupil with bad habits. His virtues of accuracy, economy and control are those most lacking today.

Essays, 247

Most men and women of genius have entertained preposterous opinions.

Ibid., 338

What our senses, unguided, perceive is far from multitudinous and diverse. We begin life in a world of practically uniform phenomena. A stretch of country to a Londoner, a street of houses to an Australian, a crowd of men and women to the bookworm, present no point of peculiarity; the trees and crops and lie of the land, the nature of the soil, require a long apprenticeship before they reveal their individual characters ... Men and women are only types until one knows them. The whole of thought and taste consists in distinguishing between similars.   *Essays*, 214

'Artists are men; men live in society and are in a large measure formed by the society in which they live. Therefore works of art cannot be considered historically except in human and ultimately in social terms.' By 'social' Mr [Anthony] Blunt, as all his colleagues, means 'economic'. It would be equally true and equally fair to say 'Men live on the earth, etc. Therefore works of art cannot be considered historically except in geographical and ultimately in meteorological terms.'
                                                    Ibid., 199

Mr Edward Upward contrasts Shakespeare's world with our own of 'class struggle and crime and war' as though he really believed that *A Midsummer Night's Dream* was the product of an age of arcadian innocence instead of an escape from a world far more savage, far more unjust than ours, perplexed by a loss of belief far wider and by social disturbances far more bitter than anything we know.
                                                    Ibid.

These savants sought a way out of their puzzlement by saying that the book could be treated 'on two levels' as though it comprised two complementary cellophane tracings, ignoring the fact that any book worth discussing at length exists in three dimensions, a solid thing which can be viewed from any angle and cut in any section. Most good novels vary in mood and method – satire, comedy, drama, allegory, analysis, description comment and criticism, all have their part. *Hemlock and After* is a singularly rich, compact and intricate artifact and ... a thing to rejoice over.   *Ibid.*, 421

Modern novelists since and including James Joyce try to represent the whole human mind and soul and yet omit its determining character – that of being God's creature with a defined purpose.
                                                    Ibid., 302

So in my future books there will be two things to make them unpopular: a preoccupation with style and the attempt to represent man more fully, which, to me, means only one thing, man in his relation to God.

Ibid.

Mgr Knox's message survives entire in black and white, as compelling in print as in his quiet, scholar's voice. His ideas, complex and seemingly incongruous, come together, fuse, and become simple, permanent and luminous. That, rather than his abounding verbal felicity, is what makes his art [of the sermon] notable.

Ibid., 371

I think it is time we made up our minds that poetry is one of the arts which has died in the last eighty years. Poets now have as much connection with poetry as the Fishmongers' Company has with selling fish. They carry on the name and the banquets but have retired from trade generations ago.

Horizon, 4 November 1941

The *Critical Essays* of Mr George Orwell represent at its best the new humanism of the common man. It is a habit of mind rather than a school. The essential difference between this and previous critical habits is the abandonment of the hierarchic principle. It has hitherto been assumed that works of art exist in an order of precedence with the great masters, Virgil, Dante and their fellows, at the top and the popular novel of the season at the bottom …. The new critics begin their inquiry into a work of art by asking: 'What kind of man wrote or painted this? What were his motives, conscious or unconscious? What sort of people like his work? Why?' With the class distinctions the great colour-bar also disappears; that hitherto impassable barrier between what was 'Literature' and what was not. Vast territories are open for exploitation.

Essays, 305

Instead of the Liberty, Equality and Fraternity of the Americas, Europe offers its artists Liberty, Diversity and Privacy. Perhaps it is for this that so many of the best American writers go abroad.

Ibid., 300

Talking films were just being introduced [in 1929], and had set back by twenty years the one vital art of the century.

Labels, 11

One had supposed that the faithful hunchback would go to the war, be wounded, and emerge from the hospital whole and handsome. This did not happen; he won a lottery and solaced himself with his gorilla, while the heroine married the wicked nobleman. For so much injustice one was grateful.

Essays, 14

A blackball for all connected with Laurence Olivier's *Hamlet*.

(*Express* Film Tribunal judgement) *Daily Express*, 3 January 1949

Charlie Chaplin is not merely unpopular in Hollywood. For many years he has been the victim of organized persecution. A community whose morals are those of caged monkeys professes to be shocked by his domestic irregularities .... Any stick is good enough to beat the man who has given more pure delight to millions than all the rest put together.

Essays, 337

Talent is sometimes forgiven in Hollywood, genius never.

Ibid.

In Southern California the film community are like monks in a desert oasis, their lives revolving about a few shrines – half a dozen immense studios, two hotels, one restaurant; their sacred texts are their own publicity and the local gossip columns. The only strangers they ever see have come to seek their fortunes. None of these will hold the mirror up to Caliban. Artists and public men elsewhere live under a fusillade of detraction and derision; they accept it as a condition of their calling. Not so in Hollywood, where all is a continuous psalm of self praise.

Ibid., 325

No one in Hollywood considers the possibility of growing up.

Ibid., 328

The Hays Office enforces a code which forbids the production of any film which can be harmful to anyone, or offend any racial or religious susceptibility. No such code is feasible in a heterogeneous society. ... Every attempt is made by innuendo to pack as much lubricious material as possible into every story, while mature dramatic works intended for a morally stable, civilized audience have their essential structure hopelessly impaired.

Ibid., 330

The affinity to the film is everywhere apparent [in Graham Greene's *The Heart of the Matter*]. It is the camera's eye which moves from the hotel balcony to the street below, picks out the policeman, follows him to his office, moves about the room from the handcuffs on the wall to the broken rosary in the drawer, recording significant detail. It is the modern way of telling a story .... Perhaps it is the only contribution the cinema is destined to make to the arts.

Ibid., 362

GRAHAM GREENE: It will be a relief not to write about God for a change.
EVELYN WAUGH: Oh? I wouldn't drop God if I were you. It would be like P.G. Wodehouse dropping Jeeves halfway through the Wooster series.

Sunday Times, 17 April 1966

Art & Architecture

In writing script, once the barest respect has been paid to the determining structure of the letter, the pen is free to flourish and elaborate as it will. In the control of these often minute variations of form ... there is scope for every talent required in the building of a cathedral.

Essays, 24

Ruskin started his pupils with a lichened twig or spray of ivy to teach them the alphabet; Mr Crease started me with the alphabet and led me to the lichened twig and the singularly lovely irises that grew in the garden of Sompting Abbotts.

Ibid.

The art of the scribe is sometimes considered spinsterish. The sweep and precision of [Edward] Johnston's strokes were as virile as a bull-fighter's and left me breathless.

Little Learning, 146

There is a doubt that arises out of M. le Corbusier's sane and courageous plan. How much confidence can we have in the stability of an economic system that has so far directed itself almost unconcernedly towards chaos? Perhaps the chief value of *Urbanisme* is as a social document which shows what the great cities of the world might have made of this decade if they had not chosen to have a war instead.

Essays, 64

Collins had exposed the fallacy of modern aesthetics to me: 'If you allow Cezanne to represent a third dimension on his two-dimensional canvas, then you must allow Landseer his gleam of loyalty in the spaniel's eye' ... but it was not until Sebastian, idly turning the pages of Clive Bell's *Art*, read: ' "Does anyone feel the same kind of emotion for a butterfly or a flower that he feels for a cathedral or picture?" Yes. I do,' that my eyes were opened.

Brideshead, 26

I do not know who started the idea of 'good taste'. I suspect that DORA* had a younger brother who went to art classes at an evening polytechnic, and that it all began with him.

Essays, 44

And if you see sarcastic glances being cast at the tinted photograph of the Acropolis or the Landseer engraving, just you say very decisively, 'I don't know much about art, but I do know what I like'; then they will see that they are beaten, and Mrs Brown will say to the vicar's wife that it is so sad you have no taste, and the vicar's wife will say to the doctor's wife that it really only shows what sort of people you are, but all three will envy you at heart and even perhaps, one by one, bring out from the attics a few of the things they really like.   *Ibid.*, 45

There seem to me few things more boring than the cult of mere antiquity …. I wish all the rectors who spend their days in scratching up flint arrow-heads and bits of pottery would bury them again and go back to their prayers.   *Labels*, 107

In the tomb of Tutankhamen we are in touch with a civilization of splendour and refinement; of very good sculpture, superb architecture, opulent and discreet ornament, and, so far as one can judge, of cultured and temperate social life, comparable upon equal terms with that of China or Byzantium or eighteenth century Europe, and superior in every artistic form to Imperial Rome or the fashionable cultures of the Minoans or the Aztecs.   *Ibid.*

Masterpieces exalt and refine and inspire, but their constant proximity can become oppressive.   *Essays*, 544

Today we need a new Ruskin to assert 'some principles of art economy.' First, that the painter must represent visual objects. Anatomy and perspective must be laboriously learned and conscientiously practised. That is the elementary grammar of his communication. Secondly, that by composition, the choice and arrangement of his visual objects, he must charm, amuse, instruct, edify, awe his fellow men, according as his idiosyncrasy directs. Verisimilitude is not enough, but it is the prerequisite. That is the lesson of the photographer's and of the abstractionist's failure.   *Ibid.*, 507

* The Defence of the Realm Act, used by the bleakly puritanical Home Secretary Sir Joynson Hicks ('Jix') to ban books, plays, mixed sunbathing … (Ed.)

It must not be thought that the plain man had – or to this day has – any natural taste for plainness. Poor fellow, it has been drummed into him by a hundred experts, writing in what are ironically termed 'home pages', that ornament is vulgar, and … his only protest is to spend longer hours among the aspidistras of the bar parlour. Left to himself, in that golden age of philistinism, he ransacked the whole animal and vegetable kingdom and the realms of geometry for decorative notions.

Ibid., 220

The huge euphoria of the Victorian home may be attributed directly to the abundance of ornament. How much of the neurotic boredom of today comes from the hygienic blankness of offices, aerodrome waiting-rooms, hospitals? The human mind requires constant minor occupations to put it at rest. The eye must be caught and held before the brain will work.

Ibid., 466

The phrase 'Victorian monstrosity' is common currency. Before it is too late, may we not consider that the rustic garden furniture, the Gothic gateposts, and the Jubilee drinking fountains, all in cast iron, gave keen pleasure at the time and therefore are almost certain to do so again?

The Times, 3 March 1942

In only one branch of painting did we produce a unique, idiosyncratic national school. That is the school of narrative composition founded by Hogarth and perfected a hundred years later …. It may be defined as the detailed representation of contemporary groups, posed to tell a story and inculcate a moral precept …. previous and subsequent events are implicit in the scene portrayed.

Essays, 502

Holman Hunt was obsessed with the structure of objects and with the exact tincture of shadows. While his contemporaries in France, whom he regarded with loathing and contempt, sought to record a glimpse, he sought to record months of intense scrutiny.   *Ibid.*, 553

Hunt rejoiced in defying contemporary standards of prettiness. Why does not the present age rejoice with him [in] the invention, accomplishment, untiring vitality and dedicated purpose of these great and often hidden masterpieces?

Ibid.

If every museum in the New World were emptied, if every famous building in the Old World were destroyed and only Venice saved, there would be enough there to fill a full lifetime with delight. Venice, with all its complexity and variety, is in itself the greatest surviving work of art in the world.

Ibid., 545

There is only one ugly building in Venice today – the campanile of St Mark's. It has stood there in defiance of proportion and elegance for 500 years.

Ibid., 547

In the present half century we have seen architects abandon all attempt at 'style' and our eyes are everywhere sickened with boredom at the blank, unlovely, unlovable facades which have arisen from Constantinople to Los Angeles.

Ibid., 478

I have always loved building, holding it to be not only the highest achievement of man but one in which, at the moment of consummation, things were most clearly taken out of his hands and perfected, without his intention, by other means … More even than the work of the great architects, I loved the buildings that grew silently with the centuries, catching and keeping the best of each generation, while time curbed the artist's pride and the Philistine's vulgarity, and repaired the clumsiness of the dull workman.

Brideshead, 198

A work of art is not a matter of thinking beautiful thoughts or experiencing tender emotions (though those are its raw materials), but of intelligence, skill, taste, proportion, knowledge, discipline and industry; especially discipline. No number of disciples can compensate for lack of that.

Spectator, 18 November 1960

Abroad

A map, and particularly one with blank spaces and dotted rivers, can influence a travelmaniac as can no book or play .... Every place in the world is worth visiting and treasures some peculiar gift for the traveller who goes there in decent humility.

Essays, 134

Seville is one of the most lovely cities I have ever seen; only a general diffidence about the superlative prevents me from saying the most lovely. I can think of many with more lovely things in them, but none that has the same sweetness and refinement combined with activity and good sense; it seems to avoid every sort of vulgarity, even that of the professional beauty.

Labels, 197

I do not think I shall ever forget the sight of Etna at sunset; the mountain almost invisible in a blur of pastel grey, glowing on the top and then repeating its shape, as though reflected, in a wisp of grey smoke, with the whole horizon behind radiant with pink light, fading gently into a grey pastel sky. Nothing I have ever seen in Art or Nature was quite so revolting.

Ibid., 169

But the glory and delight of Barcelona, which no other town in the world can offer, is the architecture of Gaudi.   *Ibid.*, 175

The two most accomplished men I met during this six months I was abroad [were] Armenians. A race of rare competence and the most delicate sensibility. They seem to me the only genuine 'men of the world'.

Remote People, 110-11

The tourist is a vile and ludicrous figure; he is always wrong. It is he who debauches the hospitality of primitive peoples, who vulgarises the great monuments of antiquity, littering cathedral squares with ice-cream stalls, the desert with luxury hotels. A comic figure, always inapt in his comments, incongruous in his appearance; romance withers before him, avarice and deceit attack him at every step; the shops that he patronizes are full of forgeries ... But *we* are travellers and cosmopolitans, the tourist is the other fellow.

Essays, 171

Mr Nesbitt's book is a fine example of pure travel literature.
He is not a professional writer on a holiday, but an explorer
whose adventures, of themselves, demand expression. ... As
the narrative becomes more direct, more austere, and
abandons any attempt at reflection and comment, it becomes
part of the journey itself, arid and exacting in places, as the
very ground he covered, almost dull, but with the dead
monotony of the trail, painful with the acute hardships his
party suffered ... the day-to-day record of hardship, danger
and loss could not be improved by any amount of fine writing.

Ibid., 139-40

The most valuable commodity for the tourist, whether he is
cruising along the French Riviera in a yacht or ploughing
through unmapped areas of virgin forest, is alcohol .... With a
glass in his hand, the tourist can gaze out on the streets of
Tangier, teeming with English governesses and retired
colonels, and happily imagine himself a Marco Polo.

Ibid., 174

The water gently spilled over [Kaieteur] as though from a
tilted dish. At the edge it was brown as the river behind it,
rapidly turning to white and half-way down dissolving in
spray so that it hung like a curtain of white drapery. It fell
sheer from its seven hundred odd feet, for the cliff had been
hollowed back in the centuries and the edge jutted over an
immense black cavern. At the foot dense columns of spray rose
to meet it so that the impression one received was that the
water slowed down, hesitated, and then began to reascend, as
though a cinema film had been reversed.

Ninety-Two Days, 216

I lay on the overhanging ledge watching the light slowly fail,
the colours deepen and disappear. The surrounding green was
of a density and intenseness that can neither be described nor
reproduced; a quicksand of colour, of shivering surface and
unplumbed depth, which absorbed the vision, sucking it down
and submerging it.

Ibid., 217

One went abroad to observe other ways of living, to eat
unfamiliar food and see strange buildings. In a few years' time
the world will be divided into zones of insecurity which one
can penetrate only at the risk of murder and tourist routes
along which one will fly to chain hotels, hygienic, costly and
second-rate.   *Essays*, 540

It is by crawling on the face of it that one learns a country; by the problems of transport that its geography becomes a reality and its inhabitants real people. Were one to be levitated on a magic carpet, one would see all that was remarkable but it would be a very superficial acquaintance, and in the same way, if one leaves the reader out of one's confidence ... one will not have given them a share in the experience of travel, for these checks and hesitations constitute the genuine flavour.

Ninety-Two Days, 210

If one is interested in one's fellow beings – and that after all is the first requisite of a novelist – one cannot neglect the study of human nature in unfamiliar surroundings.

Essays, 134

The narrative, though usually stilted and often sententious, still preserves the flavour of first hand experience – for one reader at least an unmistakable and intoxicating flavour.

Ibid., 129

Mr Gruhl's [public is] that small circle, of which the present reviewer claims membership, who prefer all but the very worst travel books to all but the very best novels.

Ibid.

'That's the way to deal with him,' said Alistair. 'Keep a stopper on the far-flung stuff.'

Black Mischief, 232

Manners & Morals

There are still things which are worth fighting *against* ...

Essays, 128

It is better to be narrow minded than to have no mind, to hold limited and rigid principles than none at all. That is the danger which faces so many people today – to have no considered opinions on any subject, to put up with what is wasteful and harmful with the excuse that 'there is good in everything'.

Ibid.

It seems to me that a prig is someone who judges people by his own, rather than by their, standards; criticism only becomes useful when it can show people where their own principles are in conflict.

Remote People, 51

The modern craze for 'converting' mews seems to me one of the most pathetic signs of of national silliness. In order to attain physical proximity to people richer than themselves, normally intelligent citizens will lurk in these wretched back alleys and pay rents which would provide them with a decent house and garden in the suburbs. Do these mews dwellers honestly think that they can maintain their dignity best by living in the stables of their economic superiors?

Daily Mail, 12 July 1930

Tipping is not a thing that has ever worried me. I like to be capricious in the matter, following no rule except my own inclination. I do not actually say, 'This is for you my good man. Do not spend it on strong drink,' but I feel rather as though I were presenting prizes at a school sports; rewards for skill and effort based on close observation of form. I regard it as a purely personal whim. *Essays*, 585

Manners are especially the need of the plain. The pretty can get away with anything. The publishers should have chosen an ugly, elderly, ill tempered woman to write their book [of etiquette]; or better, a man, for women are naturally Bohemian, while men honour convention.

Ibid., 587

There is only one way of being perfectly dressed – that is, to be grossly rich. You may have exquisite discrimination and the elegance of a gigolo, but you can never rival the millionaire if he has even the faintest inclination towards smartness. His valet wears his suits for the first three days so that they never look new, and confiscates them after three months so that they never look old. He basks in a perpetual high noon of bland magnificence.

Ibid., 54

If your object in choosing your clothes is to give an impression of wealth, you had far better adopt a pose of reckless dowdiness and spend your money in maintaining under a hat green and mildewed with age a cigar of fabulous proportions.

Ibid.

We were instructed by a man of about my age, who wore very dark blue shirts, a lemon yellow tie and horn-rimmed glasses, and it was largely by reason of this warning that I modified my own style of dress until it approximated to what my cousin Jasper would have thought suitable for country house visiting.

Brideshead, 95

There were never more bathrooms in England than there are today and never so many dirty necks and finger-nails in both sexes. Heaven knows what horrors lie hidden below the clothes. A few girls who work as mannequins are professionally clean; countless others should be sent to bed supperless.

Essays, 591

For generations we English have been the least ceremonious of nations. That was because we enjoyed complete self-confidence in our order. We preserved, behind our easy-going and eccentric ways, a basic decorum. It is time we awoke to the danger of finding ourselves a people of slatterns and louts.

Ibid., 589

The great difference between our manners and the those of the Americans (on the whole a better mannered people than ourselves) is that theirs are designed to promote cordiality, ours to protect privacy.

Ibid., 592

My father taught me that it was flagitious to leave a letter of any kind unanswered. (Indeed his courtesy was somewhat extravagant. He would write and thank people who wrote to thank him for wedding presents and when he encountered anyone as punctilious as himself the correspondence ended only with death.)

Ibid., 301

The telephone, that pernicious device, should never be used except among intimate friends and, I suppose, in commerce. I do not know how much real value it is in offices. It seemed to me to cause a great deal of misunderstanding and waste of time in the army.

Ibid., 591

The call to order I plead for is something quite superficial. A matter of style of living. In the decade before the war European fashions were set largely by homosexuals. They are naturally nonconformist and their influence was to remove almost all the formalities which still survived, but they had their own kind of elegance and standards of politeness … and most people were grateful to them for making everything so gay and ornamental.

Ibid., 589

One simple reform which is needed is the return of the habit of dressing in the evening … young men would soon learn that evening dress is perfectly comfortable and that wearing it puts them in a festive mood.

Ibid., 590

Historically ceremony and etiquette are the revolution against barbarism of peoples developing their civilization. They can also be the protection of those in decline; strong defences behind which the delicate and valuable are preserved.

Ibid., 592

Food & Drink

There is a lot about food in [Patrick Balfour's] *Grand Tour*: too much for some readers, but not too much for me.

Spectator, 7 December 1931

Mrs Beaver stood with her back to the fire, eating her morning yoghurt. She held the carton close under her chin and gobbled with a spoon.

'Heavens, how nasty this stuff is. I wish you'd take to it, John.' *Handful of Dust*, 9

'Two raw onions and a plate of oatmeal porridge,' said Lord Monomark. 'That's all I've taken for luncheon in the last eight months. And I feel two hundred per cent better – physically, intellectually and ethically.'

Black Mischief, 76

'Fed doggies in market-place. Children tried to take food from doggies. Greedy little wretches.' *Ibid.*, 160

MARCH 15TH
*Imperial Banquet for Welcoming the English
Cruelty to Animals*

MENU OF FOODS

VITAMIN A
Tin Sardines
VITAMIN B
Roasted Beef
VITAMIN C
Small Roasted Sucking Porks
VITAMIN D
Hot Sheep and Onions
VITAMIN E
Spiced Turkey
VITAMIN F
Sweet Puddings
VITAMIN G
Coffee
VITAMIN H
Jam

Ibid., 170

Adam ate some breakfast. No kipper, he reflected, is ever as good as it smells; how this too earthly contact with flesh and bone spoiled the first happy exhilaration; if only one could live, as Jehovah was said to have done, on the savour of burnt offerings. He lay back for a little in his bed thinking about the smells of food, of the greasy horror of fried fish and the deeply moving smell that came from it; of the intoxicating breath of bakeries and the dullness of buns ...

Vile Bodies, 63

'Let us see what they have been able to scrape up for luncheon.' They had scraped up fresh river fish, and stewed them with white wine and aubergines; also a rare local bird which combined the tender flavour of partridge with the solid bulk of the turkey; they had roasted and stuffed it with bananas, almonds and red peppers; also a baby gazelle which they had seethed with truffles in its mother's milk; also a dish of feathery Arab pastry and a heap of unusual fruits. Mr Baldwin sighed wistfully. 'Well,' he said, 'I suppose it will not hurt us to rough it for once. We shall appreciate the pleasures of civilisation all the more ... but my descent in the parachute gave me quite an appetite. I had hoped for something a little more enterprising.'

Scoop, 244

The ladies did not dine with the gentlemen but they dined extremely well .... The plain but abundant fare comprised oysters stewed with saffron, boiled crabs, soles fried in butter, sucking-pig seethed in milk, roast capons, titbits of lamb spitted between slices of onion, a simple sweet confection of honey and eggs and cream, and a deep Samian pitcher of home-brewed mead; it would not have done in Italy or Egypt but it was well-suited to the British ladies' taste and circumstances.

Helena, 17

After four years of war .... Ruben's restaurant was a rare candle in a dark and naughty world. Kerstie Kilbannock, who had made noxious experiments with custard powder and condiments, once asked, 'Do tell me Ruben, what is the secret of your mayonnaise?' and received the grave reply: 'Quite simple, my lady, fresh eggs and olive oil.'

Sword of Honour, 552

The cream and hot butter mingled and overflowed, separating each glaucous bead of caviar from its fellows, capping it in white and gold.

'I like a little bit of chopped onion with mine,' said Rex. 'Chap-who-knows told me it brought out the flavour.'

Brideshead Revisited (1960), 167

The soup was delicious after the rich blinis – hot, thin, bitter, frothy .... The sole was so simple and unobtrusive that Rex failed to notice it.

Ibid., 168

We ate to the music of the press – the crunch of the bones, the drip of blood and marrow, the tap of the spoon basting the thin slices of breast .... Rex smoked his first cigarette .... 'You know, the food here isn't half bad; someone ought to take this place up and make something of it.' ... After the duck came a salad of watercress and chicory in a faint mist of chives. I tried to think only of the salad.

Ibid., 168-70

For a moment Waugh's spirits were restored by the prospect of a dish of lampreys cooked with cream and brandy and port, a local speciality. 'I'm sure I shall die of a surfeit,' he said, beaming with greed. But just then he caught sight of a fellow passenger on his ship, to whom he must have taken one of his unreasonable but typically violent dislikes. 'It's no good,' he said, 'that ugly mug has put me off my grub.' He pushed his plate away and relapsed into gloom.

Daphne Fielding, *The Nearest Way Home*, 166-7

'I've got a motor-car and a basket of strawberries and a bottle of Château Peraguey – which isn't a wine you've ever tasted, so don't pretend. It's heaven with strawberries' .... On a sheep-cropped knoll under a clump of elms we ate the strawberries and drank the wine – as Sebastian promised they were delicious together ... and the sweet scent of the tobacco merged with the sweet summer scents around us and the fumes of the sweet golden wine seemed to lift us a finger's breadth above the turf and hold us suspended.

Brideshead Revisited (1960), 25-6

The white Bordeaux are strangely neglected in England and America. ... By false analogy with champagne, their sweetness, all their own and deeply scented as the rose, is held against them.

Wine in Peace and War, 58

I rejoiced in the Burgundy. It seemed a reminder that the world was an older and a better place than Rex knew .... By chance I met this same wine again, in the first autumn of the war; it had softened and faded in the intervening years but it still spoke in the pure, authentic accent of its prime, the same words of hope.
Brideshead Revisited (1960), 169

In a novel I once gave a description of two undergraduates sampling a cellar of claret. I never had that experience at that age. Indeed I do not think that at 20 I could distinguish with any certainty between claret and burgundy. Port was another matter. Many of the colleges had ample bins of fine vintages of which undergraduates were allowed a strictly limited share. Port we drank with reverence and learned to appreciate.
Essays, 611

There is some highly prized port in the senior common-room cellars that is only brought up when the College fines have reached fifty pounds. 'We shall have a week of it at least', said Mr Postlethwaite, 'a week of Founder's port.' ... 'It'll be more if they attack the Chapel', said Mr Sniggs. 'Oh, please God, make them attack the Chapel.'
Decline and Fall, 14

The heavy port drinker must be prepared to make some sacrifice of personal beauty and agility.
Wine in Peace and War, 61

Beware of the heresy that sherry is better for you than cocktails. Its only medical advantage is that one drinks far less. It is the cup that neither cheers nor inebriates.
Harper's Bazaar, November 1933

Gin is an admirable emollient for sore nerves. It should be liberally quaffed at all official gatherings where the guests are obliged to be cordial to people they never wish to see again.
Wine in Peace and War, 47

The apotheosis of medicinal drinking is the cocktail, which exists purely as a stimulant. There must be some good in the cocktail party to account for its immense vogue among otherwise sane people. Personally I have never found it. I prefer to take medicine in comparative privacy.
Ibid., 48

Wine is one of the staples of civilization and, until the sinister developments of the last quarter century, was an integral part of every home with any pretension to culture.
Ibid., 11

It is quite possible to be a connoisseur and to lack at the same time all sense of enjoyment. Many literary critics have this sorry gift. Some years ago a great wine-tasting contest in Bordeaux was, I believe, won by a man who had a particular dislike for the stuff. He was a wine waiter at a great hotel, endowed by nature with a uniquely sensitive nose and a retentive memory. No drop had ever passed his lips, but when it came to the test he was able to name the chateau and year of a dozen clarets merely by putting his nose to the glass. He was like a sanitary inspector smelling drains.

Ibid., 39

I had held that champagne was the ideal beverage for any hour of the day and night and for every physical condition. Now I am obliged to admit that the French know better and that it is a wine for (frequent) occasional use.

Essays, 635

In a corner of the kitchen they found a dozen bottles bearing the labels of various mineral waters – Evian, St Galmiet, Vichy, Malvern – all empty. It was Mr Youkoumian's practice to replenish them, when required, from the foetid well at the back of the house.

Black Mischief, 196

The cognac was not to Rex's taste. It was clear and pale and it came to us in a bottle free from grime and Napoleonic cyphers. It was only a year or two older than Rex and lately bottled. They gave it to us in very thin tulip-shaped glasses of modest size. 'Brandy's one of the things I do know a bit about', said Rex. 'This is a bad colour. What's more, I can't taste it in this thimble.' They brought him a balloon the size of his head. He made them warm it over the spirit lamp. Then he rolled the splendid spirit round, buried his face in the fumes, and pronounced it the sort of stuff he put soda in at home. So, shamefacedly, they wheeled out of its hiding place the vast and mouldy bottle they kept for people of Rex's sort. ... He lit his cigar and sat back at peace with the world; I, too, was at peace in another world than his.

Brideshead Revisited (1960), 171

Class & Society

By and large, the most valuable possession of any nation is an accepted system of classes.

Essays, 583

A shriller note could now be heard rising from Sir Alastair's rooms; any who have heard that sound will shrink at the recollection of it; it is the sound of the English county families baying for broken glass.

Decline and Fall, 1

' "God bless my soul," he said, "if it isn't Grimes of Podger's! What's all this nonsense about a court-martial?" So I told him. "H'm" he said, "pretty bad. Still it's out of the question to shoot an old Harrovian. I'll see what I can do about it." '

Ibid., 40

If it is a question of talking casually in a ship or hotel with a man who wears an old school tie and one who does not, I would always choose the latter, because one can be fairly certain in advance of what the former will say.

Daily Mail, 30 August 1930

'Grimes is not the son-in-law I should readily have chosen. I could have forgiven him his wooden leg, his slavish poverty, his moral turpitude, and his abominable features; I could even have forgiven him his incredible vocabulary, if only he had been a gentleman. I hope you do not think me a snob.'

Decline and Fall, 116

Nor am I worried at the charge of snobbery. Class consciousness, particularly in England, has been so much inflamed that to mention a nobleman is like mentioning a prostitute sixty years ago. The new prudes say, 'No doubt such people do exist but we would sooner not hear about them.' I reserve the right to deal with the kind of people I know best.

Essays, 304

I believe that inequalities of wealth and position are inevitable
and that it is therefore meaningless to discuss the advantages
of their elimination; that men naturally arrange themselves in a
system of classes; that such a system is necessary for any form
of cooperative work, more particularly the work of keeping a
nation together.   *Robbery Under Law*, 17

'What my friend needs is Class. You would say, would you
not, that a non-sectarian clergyman was the social equal of the
embalmer?' 'I certainly would, Mr Barlow. There is a very deep
respect in the American heart for ministers of religion.'

Loved One, 98

As a guide to human character, pedigrees are, I suppose, about
as valuable as horoscopes.

Essays, 496

Nowhere, except perhaps in parts of Asia, is the class structure
as subtle and elaborate as in England. Everyone in England has
a precise and particular place in the social scale and constantly
manifests the fact in habit and word. Many writers have found
a rich source in this national idiosyncrasy.

Ibid., 422

Until the grand climacteric of 1945 there existed in England an
elaborate and flexible class structure which influenced, and
often determined, all social and personal relations. It was the
growth of centuries and so complex that no foreigner and few
natives could completely comprehend it. There were
recognizable a small, heterogeneous highest class and a lowest
class scarcely larger or more homogeneous – the nomadic,
destitute, outlawed. These classes occupied an entirely
disproportionate place in our literature and, accordingly, in the
impression of ourselves which we gave to the world. Between
them lay an infinity of gradations so subtle and various that
most Englishmen were aware only of the strata immediately
below and above their own.

Ibid., 312

We live under a regime which makes it an avowed purpose ...
to produce the modern two-class state of officials and
proletariat.   *Ibid.*

Everyone has always regarded any usage but his own as either
barbarous or pedantic.

Ibid., 499

'Here's how,' said the major. 'Here's how,' said the mousy wife. 'Here's how,' said Mr Crouchback with complete serenity. But Guy could only manage an embarrassed grunt.

Sword of Honour, 45

Impotence and sodomy are socially OK but birth control is flagrantly middle-class.

Essays, 497

Mr Crouchback was quite without class consciousness because he saw the whole intricate structure of his country divided neatly into two unequal and unmistakable parts. On one side stood the Crouchbacks and certain inconspicuous, anciently allied families; on the other side stood the rest of mankind.

Sword of Honour, 40

Everything turns on 'the grand old name of gentleman'. We have no equivalent phrase in English to '*noblesse oblige*'. All precepts of manners and morals define the proper conduct of 'gentlemen'. Lord Curzon, a paragon of aristocratic usage, when, as Chancellor of the University, he was shown the menu of a proposed entertainment of the king at Balliol, remarked succinctly: 'No gentleman has soup for luncheon'; he did not say: 'No monarch ...' or 'No marquis ...' He appealed above the standards of court or castle to the most elusive standard in the world.

Essays, 498

The basic principle of English social life is that *everyone* (everyone, that is to say, who comes to the front door) *thinks he is a gentleman*. There is a second principle of almost equal importance: *everyone draws the line of demarcation immediately below his own heels*.

Ibid.

In the eyes of the world we have been equalled and often surpassed by other peoples in most of the arts of peace and war; our sole unique, historic creation is the English Gentleman.

Ibid., 313

The most dismal tendency I see is that with our class system we are fast losing all national character. It was thought absurd by many and detestable by some, but it was unique and it depended for its strength and humour and achievements on variety: variety between one town and another, one county and another; one man different from another in the same village in knowledge, habits, opinions. There were different vocabularies and intonations of speech; different styles of dress. Now all those things that gave the salt to English life and were the raw material of our arts are being dissolved.

Ibid., 539

Sharp Expressions

Mr Spender misunderstands me when he speaks of my attacking those whom I believe to be down. It was precisely because I believed Mr Auden to be so very much up that I allowed myself the pleasure of a few sharp expressions.

Letters, 120

Randolph Churchill went into hospital to have a lung removed. It was announced that the trouble was not 'malignant'. ... I remarked that it was a typical triumph of modern science to find the only part of Randolph that was not malignant and remove it. *Diaries,* 792

The only convincing recommendation of [pigeon shooting] came from one of the visitors at the Bristol who remarked that it was not cricket; but even that is only very negative praise.

Labels, 33

'That,' said Dr Fagan with some disgust, 'is my daughter.'

Decline and Fall, 32

Even on that convivial evening I could feel Brideshead emanating little magnetic waves of social uneasiness, creating, rather, a pool of general embarrassment in which he floated with log-like calm.

Brideshead, 247

The Palinurus [Cyril Connolly] plan ... [is] so full of internal contradictions that it epitomizes the confusion of all his contemporaries. This plan is not the babbling of a secondary-school pupil at a youth rally but the written words of the mature and respected leader of the English intellectuals.

Essays, 312

This is a deplorably shoddy piece of work; there is, I think, no literary vice that is not exemplified in it, and had we not the Professor's [Harold Laski's] assurance that it is 'essentially an essay, nothing more', we might well take it for something much less – a hotchpotch of miscellaneous papers written at various times for various readers ... diffuse, repetitive and contradictory. *Ibid.,* 277

The Irish ... remain the same adroit and joyless race that broke
the hearts of all who tried to help them.   *Ibid.*, 384

[Irish clergy in the United States] have lost their ancestral
simplicity without yet acquiring a modest carriage of their
superior learning or, more important, delicacy in their human
relations, or imagination, or agility of mind.   *Ibid.*, 384-5

[Irish clergy in the United States] have lost their peasant
simplicity without acquiring a modest carriage of their rather
modest learning.   Ms of previous passage

[Cardinal Bourne] combined a genuine personal humility with
an absolute confidence in all his opinions (which he believed to
have been revealed to him in prayer). He was thus singularly
disqualified from normal social intercourse.   *Knox*, 167

'From the earliest times the Welsh [said Dr Fagan] have been
looked upon as an unclean people. It is thus that they have
preserved their racial integrity. Their sons and daughters mate
freely with the sheep but not with human kind except their
own blood relations.'   *Decline and Fall*, 79-80

In a corner hung the apotheosis of bogosity – a head made in
white wire, so insignificant in form and character, so drab and
boring and inadequate that it suggested the skeleton of
phrenologist's bust. The workmanship was fairly neat and
resembled in many way the kind of barely ingenious
handicraft pursued in hospitals by the disabled, who are
anxious to employ their fingers without taxing their intellect or
senses. It was called *Tête: dessin dans l'espace*, by M. Jean
Cocteau; near it stood a magnificent sculpture by Maillol.
                                        Labels, 20

It seems one has to know Mr Auden to appreciate him.
Nothing in his written work explains the dominating position
he held. There was something, apparently, in the tone of his
voice reading his and his friends' work which greatly excited
his hearers. (After all, it was the age of Hitler.)
                                        Essays, 394

At his christening the fairy godparents showered on Mr
Spender all the fashionable neuroses but they quite forgot the
gift of literary skill .... To see him fumbling with our rich and
delicate language is to experience all the horror of seeing a
Sèvres vase in the hands of a chimpanzee.   *Ibid.*, 394-5

It is natural to the Germans to make a row. The torchlit, vociferous assemblies of the Hitler Youth expressed a national passion. It is well that this should be canalized into the life of the Church. But it is essentially un-English. We seek no 'Sieg Heils'. We pray in silence.

Ibid., 630

Time marches on and no word from the Whisker [Laura Waugh]. I hope this means that you are happily engaged or piously in retreat, not that you are dead. If you are dead please be buried in the corner of the field adjoining the village cemetery. Have a small piece cut off & consecrated. I will design the tomb on my return.

Letters, 293

I dined with Mr and Mrs Luce. He handsome, well mannered, well dressed, densely stupid. She exquisitely elegant, clever as a monkey.

Ibid., 288

One honourable course is open to Mr [Hugh] Trevor-Roper. He should change his name and seek a livelihood in Cambridge.*

Ibid., 644

One is often obliged to read dull books if one is to understand the world about one. Most of the great movements of history have been founded on dull books, but these have all, by their abstractions and syllogisms, led to sensational and world-shaking conclusions; Mr Huxley's *Ends and Means* leads only to what Mr Huxley is thinking in 1937.

Essays, 213

At first the dive-bombing was impressive, but after half an hour deadly monotonous. It was like everything German – overdone.

Diaries, 502

* Trevor-Roper later became Lord Dacre and left Oxford to become Master of Peterhouse, Cambridge. (Ed.)

The Modern World

To have been born into a world of beauty, to die amid ugliness, is the common fate of all us exiles.

Little Learning, 33

This is not the age of reformation but of defence, when every man of goodwill should devote all his powers to preserving the few good things remaining to us from our grandfathers.

Essays, 533

The future, dreariest of prospects! Were I in the saddle [of the Time Machine] I should set the engine Slow Astern. To hover gently back through centuries (not more than thirty of them) would be the most exquisite pleasure of which I can conceive.

Little Learning, 1

The obliteration of English villages ... is part of the grim cyclorama of spoliation which surrounded all English experience in this century and any understanding of the immediate past must be incomplete unless this huge deprivation of the quiet pleasures of the eye is accepted as a dominant condition.

Ibid., 33

Nina looked down and saw inclined at an odd angle a horizon of straggling red suburb; arterial roads dotted with little cars; factories, some of them working, others empty and decaying; a disused canal; some distant hills sown with bungalows; wireless masts and overhead power cables ... 'I think I'm going to be sick,' said Nina.

Vile Bodies, 199

How will this absurd little jumble of antagonizing forces, of negro rhythm and psychoanalysis, of mechanical invention and decaying industry, of infinitely expanding means of communication and an infinitely receding substance of the communicable, of liberty and inertia, how will this ever cool down and crystallise out? How shall our own age look in the fancy dress parties and charity pageants of 2030?

Labels, 40

London, that noble deer bayed and brought down and torn in pieces; the city of lamentations, ruled by Lilliputians and exploited by Yahoos, whose streets, once one of the splendours of Europe, are now fit only to serve as the promenade of pet dogs and the ashtrays for the stubs of a million typists.

Essays, 215

There was one sight, however, that was unforgettable – that of Paris lying in a pool of stagnant smoke, looking, except for the Eiffel Tower, very much like High Wycombe indefinitely extended. [It] called up all the hatred and weariness which the modern megalopolitan sometimes feels towards his own civilization. *Labels*, 14-15

I was back in the centre of the Empire, and in the spot where, at the moment, 'everyone' was going. Next day the gossip-writers would chronicle the young MP's, peers and financial magnates who were assembled in that rowdy cellar, hotter than Zanzibar, noisier than the market at Harar, more reckless of the decencies of hospitality than the taverns of Kabalo or Tabora. Why go abroad? See England first. Just watch England knock spots off the Dark Continent. I paid the bill in yellow African gold. It seemed just tribute from the weaker races to their mentors.

Remote People, 240

In time to come it is likely that we and our children will look back with increasing curiosity to the free and fecund life of Victorian England …. The railings which adorned the homes of all classes were symbols of independence and privacy valued in an age which rated liberty above equality.

The Times, 3 March 1942

Suppose, as seems most unlikely, [the motor-car] once more is rendered mobile by making the whole country into a speedway and a car-park, there will be no inducement to go anywhere because all buildings will look the same, all shops sell the same produce, all people say the same things in the same voices.

Essays, 540

I thought Rex was a sort of primitive savage, but he was something absolutely modern and up-to-date that only this ghastly age could produce. A tiny bit of a man pretending he was the whole.

Brideshead, 177

All that seeming-solid, patiently built, gorgeously ornamented structure of Western life was to melt overnight like an ice-castle, leaving only a puddle of mud; man was even then leaving his post.

When the Going Was Good, 10

I told her about monasticism because we are returning to a stage when on the supernatural plane only heroic prayer can save us and when, on the natural plane, the cloister offers a saner and more civilised life than 'the world'.

Essays, 372

Progress, as it has been understood since the eighteenth century, has proved a disappointment. For every gain there has been a compensating, even a preponderating loss. Former 'progressives' suspect that they have gained all that is attainable and are in danger of losing it, while others believe that for a century the 'spirit of the age' has been moving in the wrong direction.

Ibid., 580

Africa was heaped with all the rubbish of our own continent; mechanised transport, representative government, organised labour, artificially stimulated appetites for variety in clothes, food, and amusement ... Europe has only one positive thing which it can offer to anyone, and that is what the missionaries brought.

Remote People, 205

[Mr Pinfold's] strongest tastes were negative. He abhorred plastics, Picasso, sunbathing and jazz – everything in fact that had happened in his own lifetime.

Pinfold, 14

Most of the world's troubles seem to come from people who are too busy. If only politicians and scientists were lazier, how much happier we should all be.

Essays, 572

'I think it would be very wicked indeed to do anything to fit a boy for the modern world.'

Scott-King, 88

I can see nothing objectionable in the total destruction of the earth, provided it is done, as seems most likely, inadvertently.

Essays, 538

Journalism

It is the natural inclination of any trade to provide the public with what it wants rather than what it needs; in the sphere of economics this produces a recurrent disastrous succession of slumps and booms. In matters of the mind exactly the same process is at work. It should be the proper function of an intelligentsia to correct popular sentiments and give the call to order in times of hysteria. Instead the editors and publishers, whose job it is to exploit the intelligence of others, see it as their interest to indulge and inflame popular emotion.

Essays, 199

People now use the phrase 'without contemporary significance' to express just those works which are of most immediate importance, works which eschew barbaric extremes and attempt to right the balance of civilization.

Ibid., 200

One of the arts of successful authorship is preventing the reading public from forgetting one's name in between the times when they are reading one's books. So you have to spend half your leisure in writing articles for the papers; the editors buy these because people read your books, and people read your books because they see your articles in the papers. The rest of your leisure you have to spend in doing things which you think other people will think interesting.

Labels, 10

Yes I should be pleased to write Wyndham Lewis stuff or any other kind of 'stuff ' ... Please fix up anything that will earn me anything – even cricket criticism or mothers welfare notes.

Letters, 30

My surprise in reading the Press reports of [Haile Selassie's] coronation was not that my colleagues had allowed themselves to be slapdash about their details or that they had fallen into some occasional exaggeration of the more romantic and incongruous aspects of the affair. It seemed to me that we had been witnesses of a quite different series of events.

Remote People, 51

'Getting in first with the news' and 'giving the public what it wants', the two dominating principles of Fleet Street, are not always reconcilable.   *Ibid.*

Events in a newspaper become amusing and thrilling just in so far as they are given credence as historical facts. Anyone, sitting down for a few hours with a typewriter, could compose a paper that would be the ideal of every news-editor. He would deal out dramatic deaths in the royal family, derail trains, embroil the country in civil war, and devise savage and insoluble murders. All these things would be profoundly exciting to the reader so long as he thought they were true. If they were offered to him as fiction they would be utterly insignificant.   *Ibid.*, 52

'News is what a chap who doesn't care much about anything wants to read. And its only news until he's read it. After that it's dead. We're paid to supply news. If someone else has sent a story before us, our story isn't news.'

                                        Scoop, 91

'Why, once Jakes went out to cover a revolution in one of the Balkan capitals. He overslept in his carriage, woke up at the wrong station, didn't know any different, got out, went straight to a hotel, and cabled off a thousand-word story about barricades in the streets, flaming churches, machine guns answering the rattle of his typewriter as he wrote, a dead child, like a broken doll, spreadeagled in the deserted roadway below his window – you know. Well they were pretty surprised at his office, getting a story like that from the wrong country, but they trusted Jakes and splashed it in six national newspapers. That day every special in Europe got orders to rush to the new revolution.They arrived in shoals. Everything seemed quiet enough, but it was as much as their jobs were worth to say so. ... So they chimed in too. Government stocks dropped, financial panic – and in less than a week there was an honest to God revolution under way. There's the power of the Press for you.'   *Ibid.*, 92-3

'There are two invaluable rules for a special correspondent – Travel Light and Be Prepared. Have nothing which in case of emergency you cannot carry in your own hands. But remember that the unexpected can always happen. Little things we take for granted at home, like ... a coil of rope or a sheet of tin may save your life in the wilds. I should take some cleft sticks with you.'   *Ibid.*, 56

'With regard to Policy, I expect you already have your own views. I never hamper my correspondents in any way. ... Remember that the Patriots are in the right and are going to win. The *Beast* stands by them four-square. But they must win quickly. The British public has no interest in a war which drags on indecisively. A few sharp victories, some conspicuous acts of personal bravery on the Patriot side, and a colourful entry into the capital. That is the *Beast* Policy for the war.'

Ibid.

'They all have different policies so of course they have to give different news.'

Ibid., 90

Mr Salter's side of the conversation was limited to expressions of assent. When Lord Copper was right he said, 'Definitely, Lord Copper'; when he was wrong, 'Up to a point.'

'Let me see, what's the name of the place I mean? Capital of Japan? Yokohama isn't it?'

'Up to a point, Lord Copper.'

Ibid., 16

If one could understand [why English public opinion tolerated Mexico's confiscation of British oil properties] one would come very near to understanding all the problems that vex us today, for it has at its origin the universal, deliberately fostered anarchy of public relations and private opinions that is rapidly making the world uninhabitable.

Robbery Under Law, 3

Politics & War

Politics, everywhere destructive, have dried up Mexico, frozen it, cracked it, and powdered it to dust. In the sixteenth century human life was disordered and talent stultified by the obsession of theology; today we are plague-stricken by politics.

When the Going Was Good, 9

I was a conservative when I went to Mexico and everything I saw there strengthened my opinions.

Robbery Under Law, 16

Man is, by nature, an exile and will never be self-sufficient or complete on this earth; his chances of happiness and virtue, here, remain more or less constant through the centuries and, generally speaking, are not much affected by the political and economic conditions in which he lives; the balance of good and ill tends to revert to a norm; sudden changes of physical condition are usually ill, and are advocated by the wrong people for the wrong reasons.

Ibid.

I believe in government; that men cannot live together without rules but that these should be kept at the bare minimum of safety; that there is no form of government ordained from God as being better than any other; that the anarchic elements in society are so strong that it is a whole-time task to keep the peace. *Ibid.*, 17

Civilization is under constant assault and it takes most of the energies of civilized man to keep going at all … there is only a margin of energy left over for experiment however beneficent.

Ibid., 278

There is nothing, except ourselves, to stop our own countries becoming like Mexico. *Ibid.*, 279

Barbarism is never finally defeated; given propitious circumstances, men and women who seem quite orderly will commit every conceivable atrocity. The danger does not come merely from habitual hooligans; we are all potential recruits for anarchy. *Ibid.*

The communists ... maintain that [man's] real duty in life is to get through the largest possible amount of consumable goods and to produce those goods in the largest possible quantities so that he may consume them.

Ibid., 244

We are all conservatives but what exactly are we trying to conserve? Looking over our shoulders from the ramparts do we see the unconquered citadel already in decay?

Essays, 580

I was not brought up to regard the evasion of the police as the prime aim of education, nor has my subsequent observation of the world given me any reason to think that either the wickedest men or even the worst citizens are to be found in prison. The real enemies of society are sitting snug behind typewriters and microphones pursuing their work of destruction amid popular applause.

New Statesman, 16 October 1943

Q: 'Are you for, or against, the legal government of Spain? Are you for, or against, Franco and Fascism?'
A: I know Spain only as a tourist and a reader of the newspapers. I am no more impressed by the 'legality' of the Valencia government than are English Communists by the legality of the Crown, Lords and Commons. I believe it was a bad government, rapidly deteriorating. If I were a Spaniard I should be fighting for General Franco. As an Englishman I am not in the predicament of choosing between two evils. I am not a Fascist nor shall I become one unless it were the only alternative to Marxism. It is mischievous to suggest that such a choice is imminent.

Essays, 187

A private, ironically called a 'free' press, of the kind which flourishes in France, England and the United States – where no responsibility curbs its extravagances, where the news is merely a bait to attract attention to the advertisements – is the worst possible guide to popular sympathies.

Ibid., 192

The results of English diplomacy [regarding Abyssinia] are already apparent. Italy and Germany who in 1934 seemed irreconcilable opponents are now in close and formidable alliance. ... We all see the result and are appalled; few trouble to probe further and enquire into the false ideas which have exposed us to shame.

Ibid.

It is part of Mr Chapman's thesis that no one gains anything in war. This of course is true, absolutely. War is an absolute loss, but it admits of degrees; it is very bad to fight, but it is worse to lose.

Ibid., 200

There is a natural connection between the teaching profession and a taste for totalitarian government; prolonged association with the immature, the dangerous pleasures of over-simple exposition ... dispose even the most independent minds to shirt-dipping and saluting.

Ibid., 198

The distinctions of Left and Right are now becoming as meaningless and mischievous as the circus colours of the Byzantine Empire.

Ibid., 227

It is into the claws of this latter bogy that Mr Connolly finally surrenders himself; the cold dank pit of politics into which all his young friends have gone tobogganing; the fear of Fascism, that is the new fear of Hell to the new Quakers. It is indeed a sorry end to so much talent; the most insidious of all the enemies of promise.

Ibid., 241

I am so weary about having been consistently right in all my political predictions for ten years. It is so boring seeing it all happen for the second time after one has gone through it in imagination. For you [Nancy Mitford] & Duff & Randolph life must be all one lovely surprise after another.

Letters, 273

Just seven days earlier he had opened his morning newspaper on the headlines announcing the Russian-German alliance ... now, splendidly, everything had become clear. The enemy was at last plain in view, huge and hateful, all disguise cast off. It was the Modern Age in arms. Whatever the outcome there was a place for him in that battle.

Sword of Honour, 14-15

Russia invaded Poland. Guy found no sympathy among these old soldiers for his own hot indignation. ... 'If we are concerned with justice the Russians are as guilty as the Germans.' 'Justice?' said the old soldiers. 'Justice?'

Ibid., 29

It was just such a sunny, breezy Mediterranean day two years
before when he read of the Russo-German alliance, when a
decade of shame seemed to be ending in light and reason,
when the Enemy was plain in view ... Now that hallucination
was dissolved, like the whales and the turtles on the voyage
from Crete, and he was back after less than two years'
pilgrimage in a Holy Land of illusion in the old ambiguous
world, where priests were spies and gallant friends proved
traitor and his country was led blundering into dishonour.

Ibid., 531-2

[The Second World War] cast its heroic and chivalrous disguise
and became a sweaty tug-of-war between teams of
indistinguishable louts.

Scott-King, 5

The regime of Marshal Tito has all the characteristics of
Nazism – a secret, political police, an unscrupulous
propaganda bureau, judicial murders of political opponents,
the regimentation of children into fanatical, hero-worshipping
gangs, the arrest and disappearance of civilians for no other
reason than that they spoke English and had exchanged
civilities with British troops, the kidnapping of political
opponents on allied territory, the arrest and disappearance of a
national leader who came under safe conduct to discuss
co-operation; above all the Church is subject to persecution
aimed at its extinction; great numbers of priests whose only
offence was popular esteem have been done to death, religious
houses closed and religious associations abolished.

Essays, 283

'It is too simple to say that only the Nazis wanted war. ... It
seems to me there was a will to war, a death wish, everywhere.
Even good men thought their private honour would be
satisfied by war. They could assert their manhood by killing
and being killed. They would accept hardship in recompense
for having been selfish and lazy. Danger justified privilege. I
knew Italians – not very many perhaps – who felt this. Were
there none in England.?' 'God forgive me,' said Guy. 'I was one
of them.'

Sword of Honour, 788

In war, it is notorious, opponents soon forget the cause of their
quarrel, continue the fight for the sake of fighting and in the
process assume a resemblance to what they abhorred.

Essays, 580

We suffer most of the ills of oppression by the majority.

Ibid., 581

I have never voted in a parliamentary election. Great Britain is not a democracy. All authority emanates from the Crown. Judges, Anglican bishops, soldiers, sailors, ambassadors, the Poet Laureate, the postman and especially ministers exist by the royal will. In the last 300 years, particularly in the last hundred, the Crown has adopted what seems to me a very hazardous method of choosing advisers: popular election.

Ibid., 537

If I voted for the Conservative Party and they were elected, I should feel that I was morally inculpated in their follies – such as their choice of Regius Professors; if they failed, I should have made submission to socialist oppression by admitting the validity of popular election. I do not aspire to advise my sovereign in her choice of servants.

Ibid.

Crowned heads proverbially lie uneasy. By usurping sovereignty the people of many civilised nations have incurred a restless and frustrated sense of responsibility which interferes with their proper work of earning their living and educating their children.

Ibid.

[Mr Pinfold] maintained an idiosyncratic toryism which was quite unrepresented in the political parties of his time and was regarded by his neighbours as almost as sinister as socialism.

Pinfold, 11

War as waged by airmen and physicists against civilian populations is absolutely wrong in morals and fatuous as practical politics.

Encounter, July 1968

Religion

'Apparently Mr Prendergast has been reading a series of articles by a popular bishop and has discovered that there is a species of person called a "Modern Churchman" who draws the full salary of a beneficed clergyman and need not commit himself to any religious belief.'

Decline and Fall, 121

The view implicit in my education was that the basic narrative of Christianity had long been exposed as a myth, and that opinion was now divided as to whether its ethical teaching was of present value, a division in which the main weight went against it; religion was a hobby which some people professed and others did not; at best it was slightly ornamental, at the worst it was the province of 'complexes' and 'inhibitions' – catch words of the decade – and of the intolerance, hypocrisy, and sheer stupidity attributed to it for centuries. No one had ever suggested to me that these quaint observances expressed a coherent philosophic system and intransigent historical claims; nor, had they done so, would I have been much interested.

Brideshead, 77

It only remained to examine the historic and philosophic grounds for supposing the Christian revelation to be genuine. I was fortunate enough to be introduced to a brilliant and holy priest who undertook to prove this to me, and so on firm intellectual conviction but with little emotion I was admitted into the Church.

Essays, 366-7

Campion makes the claim, which lies at the root of all Catholic apologetics, that the Faith is absolutely satisfactory to the mind, enlisting all knowledge and all reason in its cause; that it is completely compelling to any who give it 'indifferent and quiet audience'.

Campion, 120

In the present phase of European history the essential issue is no longer between Catholicism, on one side, and Protestantism, on the other, but between Christianity and Chaos.

Essays, 103

So great was the inherited subconscious power of Christianity that it was nearly two centuries before the real nature of the loss of faith became apparent. Today we can see it as the active negation of all that western culture has stood for. Civilization … came into being through Christianity, and without it has no significance or power to command allegiance.

Ibid., 104

Elsewhere a first interest in the Catholic Church is often kindled in the convert's imagination by the splendours of her worship in contrast with the bleakness and meanness of the Protestant sects. In England the pull is all the other way. The mediaeval cathedrals and churches, the rich ceremonies that surround the monarchy, the historic titles of Canterbury and York, the social organization of the country parishes, the traditional culture of Oxford and Cambridge, the liturgy composed in the hey-day of English prose style – all these are the property of the Church of England, while Catholics meet in modern buildings, often of deplorable design, and are usually served by simple Irish missionaries.

Ibid., 366

England was Catholic for nine hundred years, then Protestant for three hundred, then agnostic for a century. The Catholic structure still lies lightly buried beneath every phase of English life.

Ibid., 367

At Debra Lebanos I suddenly saw the classical basilica and the open altar as a great positive achievement, a triumph of light over darkness consciously accomplished, and I saw theology as a science of simplification by which nebulous and elusive ideas are formalised and made intelligible and exact. I saw the Church of the first century as a dark and hidden thing; legionaries off duty slipping furtively out of barracks, greeting each other by signs and passwords in a locked upper room in the side street of some Mediterranean seaport; slaves at dawn creeping from the grey twilight into the candle-lit, smoky chapels of the catacombs. … And I began to see how these obscure sanctuaries had grown, with the clarity of the Western reason, into the great open altars of Catholic Europe, where Mass is said in a flood of light, high in the sight of all.

Remote People, 88

'*Odi profanum vulgus et arceo.*' That was an echo from the old, empty world. There was no hate in [Helena] now and nothing round her was quite profane. ... She was in Rome as a pilgrim and she was surrounded by friends. ... The intimate family circle of which she was a member bore no mark of kinship. The barrow-boy grilling his garlic sausages, the fuller behind his reeking public pots, the lawyer or the lawyer's clerk, might each and all be one with the Empress Dowager in the Mystical Body. ... There was no mob, only a vast multitude of souls, clothed in a vast variety of bodies, milling about in the Holy City, in the See of Peter.

Helena, 145-6

Catholicism is a faith which, within its structure, allows of measureless diversity; the spacious wisdom of St Thomas More, the anxiety about liturgical colours of the convert spinster, the final panic of the gangster calling for the sacraments in the condemned cell, the indignation of the Irish priest contemplating the spread of mixed bathing in his parish, the ingenious proofs of the Parisian aesthete that Rimbaud was at heart a religious poet ... they are all part of the same thing.

Robbery Under Law, 208

To his own, and to each succeeding generation, Campion's fame has burned with unique warmth and brilliance; it was his genius to express, in sentences that have resounded across the centuries, the spirit of chivalry in which [the Elizabethan martyrs] suffered.

Campion, 206

In fragments and whispers we get news of other saints in the prison camps of Eastern and South-eastern Europe, of cruelty and degradation more savage than anything in Tudor England, of the same, pure light shining in darkness, uncomprehended. The haunted, trapped, murdered priest is our contemporary and Campion's voice sounds to us across the centuries as though he were walking at our elbow.

Campion (1947), viii

One of the things which inspires [the Catholic visitor to the United States] most is the heroic fidelity of the Negro Catholics ... who so accurately traced their Master's road amid insult and injury.

Essays, 383

Mr Bruce Barton says: 'The cemeteries of the world cry out man's utter hopelessness in the face of death. Here in Forest Lawn Memorial Park sorrow sees no ghastly monuments but only life and hope.' The Christian visitor might here remark that by far the commonest feature of other graveyards is still the Cross, a symbol in which previous generations have found more Life and Hope than in the most elaborately watered evergreen shrub.

Ibid., 332

[In the Church of the Holy Sepulchre] one has been at the core of one's religion. It is all there, with its human faults and superhuman triumphs, and one fully realizes, perhaps for the first time, that Christianity did not strike its first root at Rome or Canterbury or Maynooth, but here in the Levant where everything is inextricably mixed and nothing is assimilated .... Our Lord was born into a fiercely divided civilization and so it has remained. But our hope must always be for unity, and as long as the Church of the Sepulchre remains a single building, however subdivided, it forms a memorial to that essential hope.

Ibid., 420

Everything about the new religion was capable of interpretation, could be refined and diminished; everything except the unreasonable assertion that God became man and died on the Cross; not a myth or an allegory; true God, truly incarnate, tortured to death at a particular moment in time, at a particular geographical place, as a matter of plain historical fact. [Helena turned] the eyes of world back to the planks of wood on which their salvation hung.

Ibid., 410

What we can learn from Helena is something about the workings of God; that He wants a different thing from each of us, laborious or easy, conspicuous or quite private, but something which only we can do and for which we were each created.

Ibid.

To every man, however learned or devout, there come occasions when he hears a familiar dogma or precept as though for the first time .... Faith expands year by year as some formulary, long implicitly accepted, suddenly takes life and becomes a matter of urgent practical importance. To strike these lights in the mind is Ronald Knox's highest gift.

Ibid., 371

The malice of Sloth lies not merely in the neglect of duty
(though that can be a symptom of it) but in the refusal of joy.
… Sloth is the condition in which a man is fully aware of the
proper means of his salvation and refuses to take them because
the whole apparatus of salvation fills him with tedium and
disgust.

Ibid., 573

Edith Stein's spirit shines out, very clear and lonely; a brilliant
intelligence; a pure, disciplined will; a single motive power, the
Grace of God. The circumstances of her death touch us for they
lie at the heart of contemporary disaster. The aimless
impersonal wickedness which could drag a victim from the
holy silence of Carmel and drive her, stripped and crowded, to
the death chamber and the furnace, still lurks in the darkness.
But Edith's death is perhaps an irrelevant horror. Her life was
completed in Carmel. She did not sit, waiting on God. She
went out alone and by the God-given light of her intelligence
and strength of purpose, she found him.

Ibid., 435

Father Sheerin suggests that Catholic conservatism is the
product of the defensive policy necessary in the last century. I
would ask him to consider that the function of the Church in
every age has been conservative – to transmit undiminished
and uncontaminated the creed inherited from its predecessors.
Not 'is this fashionable notion one that we should accept?' but
'is this dogma the Faith as we received it?' has been the
question at all General Councils.

Ibid., 629

'Participation' in the Mass does not mean hearing our own
voices. It means God hearing our voices. I believe, to compare
small things with great, that I 'participate' in a work of art
when I study and love it silently.

Ibid., 630

Medical science has oppressed us with a new huge burden of
longevity. It is in that last undesired decade, when passion is
cold, appetites feeble, curiosity dulled and experience has
begotten cynicism, that *accidia* lies in wait as the final
temptation to destruction.

Ibid., 576

'You [the Magi] are my especial patrons,' said Helena, 'and patrons of all late-comers, of all who have a tedious journey to make to the truth, of all who are confused with knowledge and speculation, of all who through politeness make themselves partners in guilt, of all who stand in danger by reason of their talents. ... For His sake who did not reject your curious gifts, pray always for the learned, the oblique, the delicate. Let them not be quite forgotten at the Throne of God when the simple come into their kingdom.'

Helena, 240

I think what you need is a straight catechism. Who made you? Why did he make you? Whom are you addressing in prayer? Christ said: 'Ask in my name.' Who was he? Christianity is an historical religion based on certain events in time and space. Without that certainty (or as Pascal thought probability) prayer becomes merely a mood. You must get the basic grammar of the Faith. You don't need tenderness – you have been surrounded with that all your life – but instruction.

Stitch, 310